Fact Finders®

WHAT YOU NEED TO KNOW ABOUT
CANCER

CHRIS FOREST

CONSULTANT:
DR MARJORIE J. HOGAN

raintree
a Capstone company — publishers for children

Raintree is an imprint of Capstone Global Library Limited, a company incorporated in England
and Wales having its registered office at 7 Pilgrim Street, London, EC4V 6LB – Registered company number: 6695582

www.raintree.co.uk
myorders@raintree.co.uk

Developed and Produced for Raintree by Focus Strategic Communications, Inc.
  Adrianna Edwards: project manager
  Ron Edwards: editor
  Rob Scanlan: designer and compositor
  Mary Rose MacLachlan: media researcher
  Francine Geraci: copy editor and proofreader
  Wendy Scavuzzo: fact checker

ISBN 978 1 474 70396 3
19 18 17 16 15
10 9 8 7 6 5 4 3 2 1

Printed and bound in China.

British Library Cataloguing in Publication Data
A full catalogue record for this book is available from the British Library.

Photo Credits
2014 The Skin Cancer Foundation, 19; Alamy: Keith Morris, 5; Alex's Lemonade Stand Foundation, 29 (middle); Glow Images:
Corbis/Wolfgang Flamisch, 20; iStockphoto: MachineHeadz, 12 (bottom); Newscom: Blend Images/ERproductions Ltd, 12 (top),
UPI/Bill Greenblatt, 28 (top); Science Source: 3D4Medical, 8, CAMR/A. Barry Dowsett, 6 (inset), David Scharf, 6 (back), Girand, 18,
Larry Mulvehill, 11 (right), Steve Gschmeissner, 15, Sue Ford, 7, Zephyr, 16; Shutterstock: A and N Photography, 13, Alex Luengo,
17, Alexander Raths, 10, Andrey Starostin, 9 (bottom right), Binh Thanh Bui, 9 (bottom left), Bullstar, 4 (right), everything possible
(background), back cover and throughout, frantab, 21, isak55, cover (top), 1 (top), 3 (back) and throughout, Jovan Mandic, 22,
Jovan Vitanovski, cover (bottom), 1 (bottom), Kumpol Chuansakul, 11 (left), Monkey Business Images, 4 (left), Peter Zijlstra, 9 (top
middle), PhotoSkech, 23, prudkov, 25, spafra, 9 (top right), Suslik1983, 9 (top left), Vectomart, 24, vetpathologist, 14, vinz89, 29 (top),
wavebreakmedia, 27; SuperStock: Fancy Collection, 26

Every effort has been made to contact copyright holders of material reproduced in this book. Any omissions will be rectified in
subsequent printings if notice is given to the publisher.

All the internet addresses (URLs) given in this book were valid at the time of going to press. However, due to the dynamic nature
of the internet, some addresses may have changed, or sites may have changed or ceased to exist since publication. While the author
and publisher regret any inconvenience this may cause readers, no responsibility for any such changes can be accepted by either the
author or the publisher.

CONTENTS

CHAPTER 1
WHAT IS CANCER?

A doctor in a hospital tests new medicines on patients. A researcher in a laboratory begins work on a new treatment. A group of people walk 42 kilometres (26 miles) together to help raise awareness. Three siblings open a lemonade stand to raise money for a cure.

▼ Doctors test new cancer medicines.

▲ A scientist searches for cancer treatments.

What do these people have in common? They are all working to find a way to cure cancer. Their efforts will help patients to fight the disease. They will also help to find ways to put an end to cancer.

▲ People walk and run to raise money for cancer research.

DEFINING CANCER

Most people think of cancer as one disease. It is really a group of diseases that affects the **cells** of the body. Cells are the building blocks of every part of the body. Cells usually grow in the body and are replaced as they wear out.

A healthy body can start and stop cell growth. But sometimes, the body is unable to stop cell growth. This illness is called cancer. When a person has cancer, cells in a part of his or her body grow and divide much faster than usual.

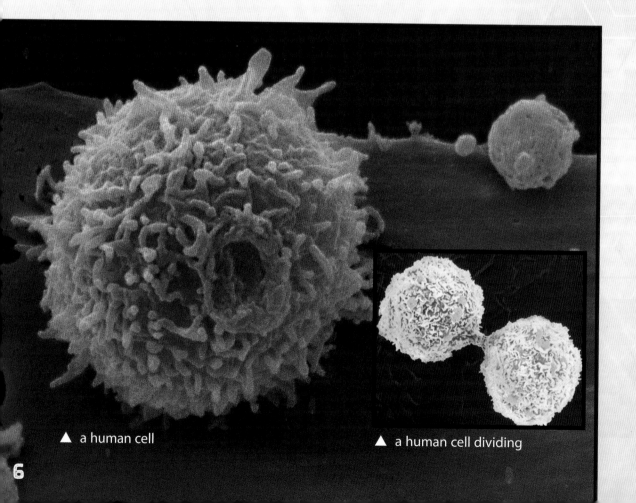

▲ a human cell

▲ a human cell dividing

At times, these cells can grow into a mass of cells. This is sometimes called a **tumour**. This uncontrolled cell growth can cause damage to cells in **tissue**, and destroy normal cells.

▼ damaged cells in tissue

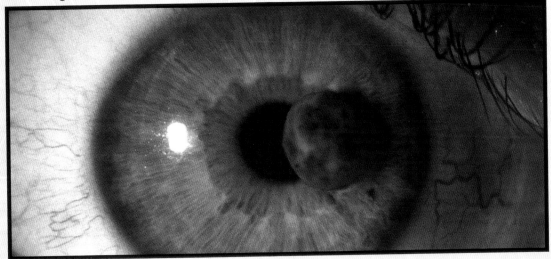

cell smallest unit of a living thing

tumour unhealthy mass of cells in the body

tissue mass of cells that form a certain part or organ of a person, animal or plant

CAUSES OF CANCER

Cancer affects many people. In the UK, more than 300,000 new cases are **diagnosed** each year. More than 1,500 of those cases are in children. Worldwide about 160,000 new cases of cancer are diagnosed in children under the age of 15 each year.

No one knows what causes this cell growth, but two facts are certain. Firstly, cancer is not a germ that can be passed through the air. Secondly, no one can catch cancer from another person.

Scientists think that cancer can be caused by damage to a person's **DNA**.

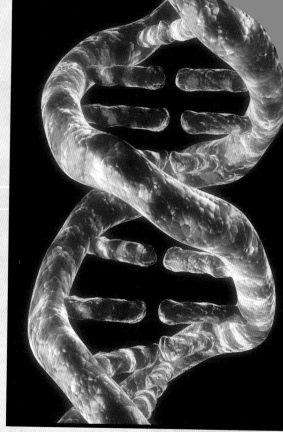

▲ human DNA

This is the material in a person's **genes** that makes each person one of a kind. Many things can cause this damage. Some causes might come from the environment. For example, chemicals in the ground, air or water may cause cancer.

diagnose find the cause of a problem

DNA material in cells that gives people their individual characteristics; DNA stands for deoxyribonucleic acid

gene tiny unit of a cell that determines the characteristics that a baby gets from his or her parents

Habits that people may have can also lead to cancer. These habits can include smoking, eating many unhealthy foods, drinking too much alcohol and lack of exercise. Sometimes the genes a person gets from a parent can make him or her more likely to get a certain type of cancer. A person might get cancer later in life if the genes change or are damaged.

▲ blueberries

▲ spinach

▲ tomatoes

HEALTH FACT

Scientists think some foods help to prevent cancer. These foods include apples, blueberries, cherries, cranberries, grapefruit, grapes, broccoli, dark leafy greens, squash, tomatoes, dried beans and legumes, flax seed, garlic, green tea, soya, walnuts and whole grains.

▲ broccoli

▲ cherries

CHAPTER 2
DIAGNOSING CANCER

Doctors carry out tests to find out if a person has cancer. Diagnosing cancer is the first step in treating it.

Special doctors focus on the treatment and care of cancer. They can come up with a plan for dealing with cancer.

▲ A doctor discusses test results and a treatment plan for cancer with her patient.

Different tests can help to diagnose cancer. A blood test can show if there are cancer cells in the blood.

Doctors may also use X-rays to tell if a person has cancer. One X-ray machine is called a **CT/CAT scan**. This machine can take 3-D images. This helps a doctor to see tissues inside the body.

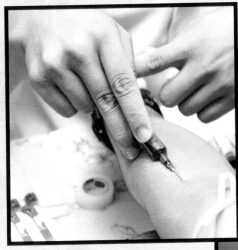

▲ A blood test can be used to diagnose cancer.

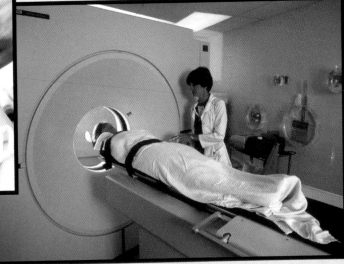

▲ Doctors also use CT scans to find out if a patient has cancer.

CT/CAT scan X-ray machine that takes pictures of the inside of a person's body; CT stands for computerized tomography

OTHER WAYS TO DIAGNOSE CANCER

Another way to tell if someone has cancer is by using an **MRI machine**. This machine can find cancer in tissues that other machines may miss.

HOW DOES AN MRI WORK?

An MRI machine looks like a long tube. Patients are injected with a dye. This dye helps organs show up more clearly when the machine scans them. An MRI machine has a very large magnet. It weighs more than 0.9 tonnes! It uses the magnet to take pictures. The MRI scan shows amazing images of the inside of the body.

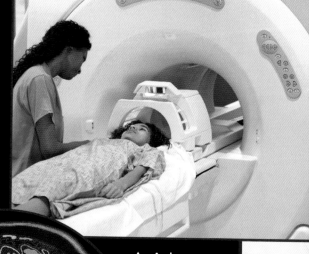

▲ A doctor prepares a patient for an MRI scan.

◀ an MRI scan showing the brain

When a doctor finds a tumour, he or she must determine if it is cancerous. To do this a doctor may take a sample of the cell tissue. This tissue is later studied, sometimes under a microscope. This process is called a **biopsy**.

▲ Doctors use microscopes to examine biopsies.

ZACH'S DIAGNOSIS

When Zach was two years old, his parents noticed he was not eating or sleeping well, and his stomach was sticking out. They took him to see the doctor. Doctors ran tests to help find out what was wrong. The tests used X-rays and CT scans together. The doctors found a tumour, and a biopsy showed it was cancerous. Zach's doctors were able to use different treatments to shrink the tumour. Doctors often use several treatments in cancer care.

MRI machine machine that uses a magnet to help take a picture of the inside of a person

biopsy taking a sample of tissue to determine if it has a disease

TYPES OF CANCER

There are different types of cancer. Some cancers begin in **organs**, **glands** and on the skin. Others form in tissues that join parts of the body, such as muscles, bones or blood vessels. Some grow in the blood system.

Cancers that affect organs include lung cancer, skin cancer, colon cancer and breast cancer. Different cancers affect organs in different ways. This means lung cancer acts differently from colon cancer, for example.

Cancers that form in the blood and bones are called leukaemia. People who have this disease have white blood cells that do not act properly. Normal white blood cells help fight illnesses. Leukaemia causes the body to have too many white blood cells that do not work the way they should.

▼ Leukaemia cells are shown in a blood sample. People who have leukaemia cannot fight infections very well.

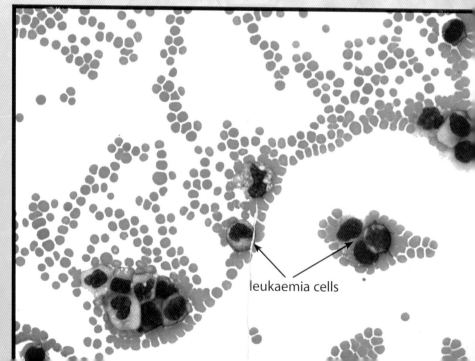

leukaemia cells

ALIJAH'S FIGHT WITH LEUKAEMIA

When Alijah was two years old, he suddenly stopped walking. Instead, he returned to crawling. After many tests, doctors were puzzled. Then they did a biopsy and found that Alijah had a type of leukaemia. Alijah's leukaemia could be treated with medicines. It had an 80 per cent cure rate. The treatments took months, but they were successful. In time, Alijah learned how to walk again.

Lymphoma is a cancer that forms in the glands of the **lymph system**. It occurs when white blood cells multiply very quickly. These cells help the body to fight infection. But too many of these cells can make you ill.

▲ lymphoma cancer cells

Parts of the body affected by the lymph system

tonsils	liver	lymph nodes	skin
heart	bone marrow	lungs	
spleen	intestines	thymus	

organ body part, such as the heart or lungs, that does a certain job

gland organ that either produces chemicals or allows substances to leave the body

lymph system body system that helps to keep body fluids balanced and to fight infections

CHAPTER 3

TREATING CANCER

After a person is diagnosed with cancer, doctors must find a way to treat it. First they need to see where the cancer is. Doctors locate the cancer using different methods, such as MRI or CT scans.

▼ This MRI scan of the brain shows cancer cells.

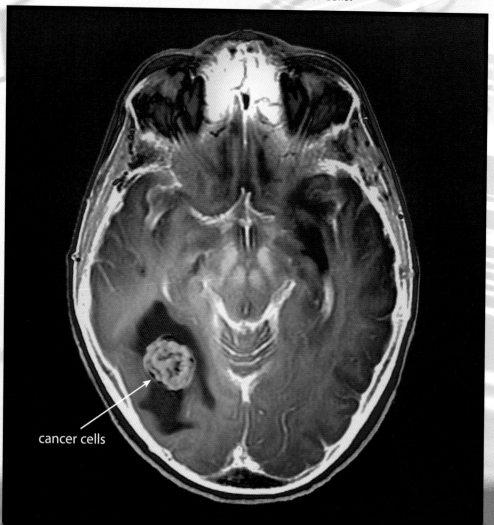

cancer cells

Next the doctors must work out how far the cancer has spread. When they find out, they label it with a stage. Cancers run from Stage 1 to Stage 4. Stage 4 cancers have spread the most.

Once doctors know the type, location and stage of the cancer, they make a plan to treat it. They may use surgery, chemicals or radiation. Often they use more than one type of treatment.

STAGES OF CANCER

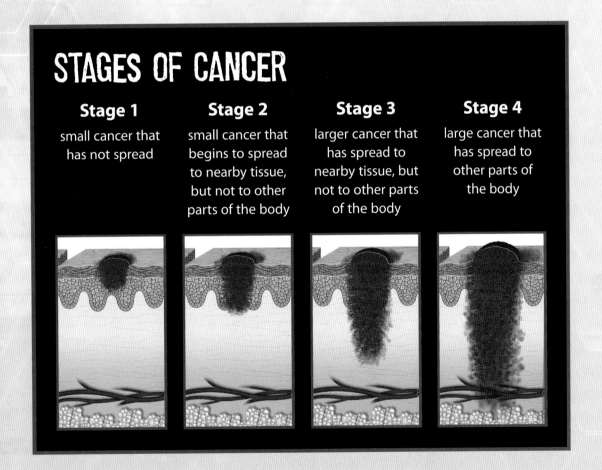

Stage 1
small cancer that has not spread

Stage 2
small cancer that begins to spread to nearby tissue, but not to other parts of the body

Stage 3
larger cancer that has spread to nearby tissue, but not to other parts of the body

Stage 4
large cancer that has spread to other parts of the body

SURGERY

Surgery is the most common way to treat cancer. If the cancer has not spread, surgery is one of the best ways to remove it. Depending on the type of cancer surgery, doctors may give patients medicine to make them sleep during the operation.

Sometimes cancer is found on the skin. The doctor can give the patient medicine to make that part of the skin numb. Then the cancer can be removed.

Doctors try to remove all cancer cells during the operation. This can stop cancer from spreading. Sometimes doctors use surgery and other cancer-fighting methods.

▼ cancer on the ear

DIFFERENCES BETWEEN NON-CANCEROUS AND CANCEROUS MOLES

Sometimes a doctor will remove growths that may not yet show signs of cancer. For example, if the doctor thinks a mole could turn into cancer, it may be removed.

Non-cancerous mole

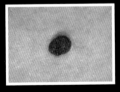
both halves are the same

borders are even

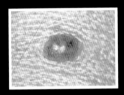
one shade of colour

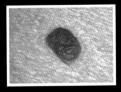
smaller than 6 millimetres

Cancerous mole

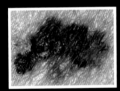
both halves are not the same

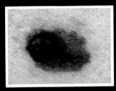
borders are uneven

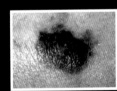
two or more shades of colour

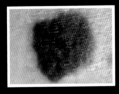
larger than 6 millimetres

CHEMOTHERAPY

Doctors may also treat cancer with chemicals. This is called **chemotherapy**. More than 80,000 people in the UK undergo chemotherapy each year.

There are about 100 medicines that can keep cancers from growing. There are two types of chemotherapy. One type is given as a pill or an injection. The other type is given through an IV line. This is a tube that puts medicine into a person's body. The tube is often placed in a vein in the arm. The IV line may also be placed in other areas of the body, such as in the chest.

The doctor makes a plan for the cancer patient's chemotherapy. The plan includes times when a patient gets treatment. It also has times when the patient rests between treatments. The treatment may last days, weeks or months.

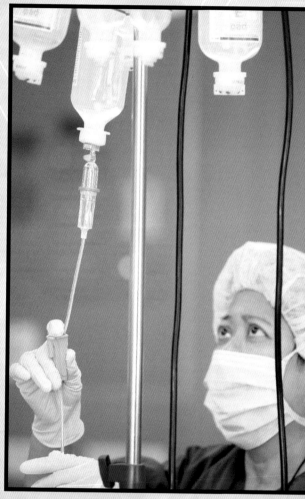

▲ A doctor adjusts IV equipment.

chemotherapy treatment of disease, such as cancer, using chemicals

SARAH, THE SURVIVOR

Sarah found out she had cancer when she was in Year 5. When doctors decided to treat it with chemotherapy, Sarah's mother sprang into action. She held a hair-cutting party to deal with Sarah's hair loss. This helped Sarah's friends get used to seeing her with short hair. It took some time, but Sarah's hair did fall out. Sarah got used to that.

Other things changed, too, such as Sarah's taste buds. Everything began to taste like metal. She did not want to eat. She also became tired and took lots of naps. But she never gave up. After some treatment, Sarah learned that her cancer had shrunk. Finally the cancer disappeared. Sarah's taste buds returned to normal, and her hair grew back!

Side effects of chemotherapy

tiredness	sore mouth
hair loss	lack of appetite
nausea	

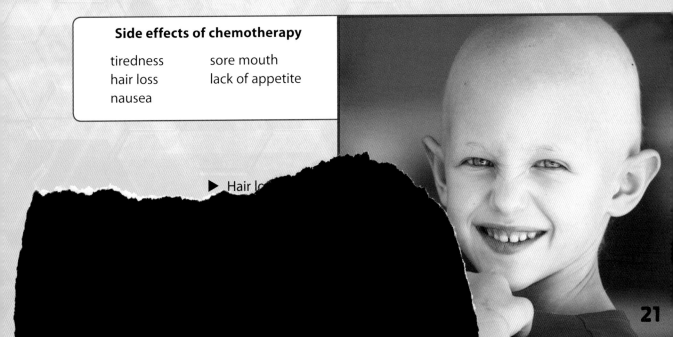

▶ Hair l

RADIATION

Radiation is another cancer treatment. It is used on about 50 per cent of all cancer patients. Radiation is energy that comes from machines such as X-ray machines. This energy is powerful enough to slow or stop cells from growing. Radiation damages normal cells and cancer cells. Normal cells can usually repair themselves, while cancer cells cannot.

Radiation can be given in two ways. Some people receive a beam of radiation on the part of their body affected by cancer. Other people may have radioactive material placed inside their body near a cancer. The material can be solid or liquid.

▼ radiation treatment for a cancer tumour

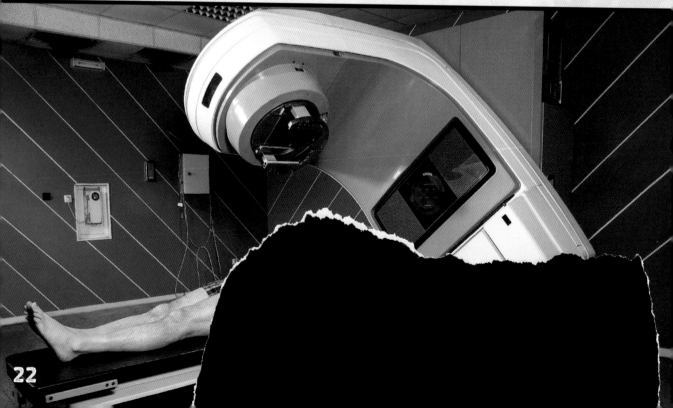

NEW FRONTIERS IN CANCER MEDICINES

Holistic medicine goes beyond just treating a person for cancer. This type of treatment focuses on the whole person – mentally, physically and socially. It includes helping the person to eat more healthily and to deal with stress. This makes the person's body, spirit and mind feel better.

Vaccines help to prevent viruses. Some are being developed today that can treat cancers people already have, or help to keep them from getting certain types of cancer in the future.

In the future we may be able to fight cancer with blood cell treatments. The patient's blood would be removed and treated to grow cancer-fighting cells. The treated blood would then be returned into the person's body to help fight the cancer.

▼ Some people practise yoga to deal with stress caused by cancer.

CHAPTER 4

FIGHTING CANCER

Fighting cancer is tough. Treatments require time and a lot of energy.

But the things most people notice are the side effects of the treatments. Different treatments have different side effects. Some side effects can be physical, and others can be emotional.

PHYSICAL SIDE EFFECTS

When people have chemotherapy, they may experience differences in their body. Some may lose their appetite. Or they may lose their hair. Patients may also develop rashes and have sore throats. Some get swollen hands and feet. Some have nail and skin problems.

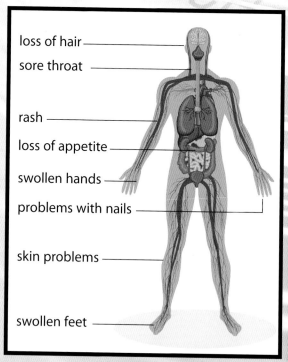

loss of hair

sore throat

rash

loss of appetite

swollen hands

problems with nails

skin problems

swollen feet

▲ physical side effects of cancer treatment

EMOTIONAL SIDE EFFECTS

Cancer patients also must deal with different emotions during treatment. They may feel tired. They may feel worried and depressed. They may feel sad or angry. They may feel nervous. It is normal to have such emotions. It is important for patients to talk about these feelings.

Emotional side effects of cancer treatment		
tiredness	depression	anger
anxiety/worry	sadness	nervousness

▼ Being sad or depressed is normal during cancer treatment.

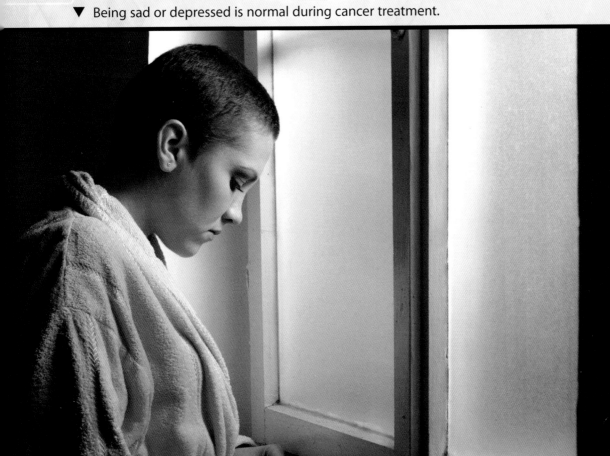

COPING WITH CANCER

People who have cancer often need help to cope with their illness. Sometimes they may feel alone. Friends and family members may be afraid to talk to them or may avoid them altogether. But people with cancer need the support of their friends and family more than ever.

▼ Family support is important during cancer treatment.

People who have cancer should ask questions about their disease. They should also talk about their feelings. Cancer patients can join groups with other people who have been treated for cancer. These support groups allow cancer patients to meet people who have had similar experiences.

▶ Support groups help people to cope with cancer.

SHANON'S STORY

In 1991, Shanon was in Year 9 when she found out she had cancer. Coping proved to be a big challenge. Shanon had many treatments and felt tired all the time. She missed many of the events she had looked forward to, such as her school play. However things changed when she joined a group for children with cancer. She found that spending time with others who knew what she was going through helped her to cope. It proved to be her "bright spot". In time she beat cancer. The experience led her to become a nurse.

MAKING A DIFFERENCE

Amazing things have been done to help fight cancer around the world. Part of the success is due to people who raise money for cancer research. Special walks, marathons and other fundraisers have raised billions of pounds for cancer research. This money goes to hospitals and research labs where cancer treatments are tested and improved.

▼ Breast cancer survivors march at an annual race in St Louis, USA.

Raising money is the first step towards finding a cure for cancer. People can help to end cancer by learning more, helping others to cope and raising awareness. In the end, everyone benefits. With each pound raised, scientists come closer to new cures for cancer.

▲ breast cancer awareness ribbon

▲ Alexandra Scott

ALEX'S LEMONADE STAND

Alex's Lemonade Stand is a US charity started by Alexandra Scott. She was diagnosed with cancer just before her first birthday. As she grew, she received many treatments. She also vowed to raise money to help other children with cancer. When she was 4 years old, Alex started her first lemonade stand with her brother. They raised about £1,300. This is one way ordinary people are making a difference in the search for a cure for cancer.

Alex passed away in 2004. She was 8 years old. She had helped to raise more than £665,000. Her supporters around the world continue her legacy through Alex's Lemonade Stand Foundation.

GLOSSARY

biopsy taking a sample tissue to determine if it has a disease

cell smallest unit of a living thing

chemotherapy treatment of disease, such as cancer, using chemicals

CT/CAT scan X-ray machine that takes pictures of the inside of a person's body; CT stands for computerized tomography

diagnose find the cause of a problem

DNA material in cells that gives people their individual characteristics; DNA stands for deoxyribonucleic acid

gene tiny unit of a cell that determines the characteristics that a baby gets from his or her parents

gland organ that either produces chemicals or allows substances to leave the body

lymph system body system that helps to keep body fluids balanced and to fight infections

MRI machine machine that uses a magnet to help take a picture of the inside of a person; MRI stands for magnetic resonance imaging

organ body part, such as the heart or lungs, that does a certain job

tissue mass of cells that form a certain part or organ of a person, animal or plant

tumour unhealthy mass of cells in the body

BOOKS

Cells and Disease (Investigating Cells), Barbara Ann Somervill (Raintree, 2011)

Health and Disease: From Birth to Old Age (Your Body For Life), Louise Spilsbury (Raintree, 2013)

Marie Curie (Against the Odds), Claire Throp (Raintree, 2015)

Stories About Surviving Cancer (Real Life Heroes), Jane Bingham (Franklin Watts, 2010)

The Usborne Complete Book of the Human Body, Anna Claybourne (Usborne Publishing Ltd, 2013)

WEBSITES

www.clicsargent.org.uk/content/children

The CLIC Sargent website contains help and support for children who want to know more about cancer.

www.gosh.nhs.uk/children

The website of Great Ormond Street Hospital for Children includes lots of information about cancer and other diseases.

INDEX